William Clifton Daland

**The Song of Songs**

William Clifton Daland

**The Song of Songs**

ISBN/EAN: 9783337181062

Printed in Europe, USA, Canada, Australia, Japan

Cover: Foto ©Lupo / pixelio.de

More available books at **www.hansebooks.com**

# THE SONG OF SONGS

## TRANSLATED FROM THE HEBREW

## WITH OCCASIONAL NOTES.

BY

## THE REV. WILLIAM C. DALAND, A. M.,

PASTOR OF THE

*FIRST SEVENTH-DAY BAPTIST CHURCH,*

LEONARDSVILLE, N. Y.

———

*SECOND EDITION.* 1888.

TO
MY WIFE.

ורחק מפנינים מכרה ׃

# PREFACE

TO THE FIRST EDITION.

This translation in its present form was prepared in connection with the series of lectures on the Old Testament, delivered by the author to his own congregation during the present summer. It is his object to exhibit the ethical purpose of the Song of Songs and to justify its place in the inspired Literature of Wisdom. He deems it the product of that Hebrew school of thought begun by those wise men gathered about Solomon—the school which produced Job and Ecclesiastes.

While recognizing the dramatic form of the poem, the translator has endeavored to preserve as simple a plan as possible consistent with the aim in view. May his work aid in the understanding of a most beautiful, though much neglected and abused part of the Divine Word.

In conclusion, the translator must acknowledge his indebtedness to the lectures of the Rev. Charles A. Briggs, D. D., of the Union Theological Seminary.

WILLIAM C. DALAND.

The Parsonage, Leonardsville, N. Y., July, 1887.

# Preface

The first edition of this version of the Song of Songs was issued in the form of a pamphlet, and intended originally for only a narrow circle of readers; but the demand for the translation from many quarters has caused the author to venture the hope that the re-publication of the same with more detailed annotations might meet with a favorable reception from Biblical students. The version has been materially improved, and many errors which appeared in the former imprint have been corrected. To the text there has been prefixed a brief introduction setting forth more particularly the intent and character of the poem. It has not been the object of the translator to make a critical commentary upon every word, nor to attempt a detailed exposition of the book. He has simply called attention to those passages in which the rendering is different from that of most interpreters, or those passages which concern either the dramatic arrangement or what the translator conceives to be the ethical purpose of the poem.

WILLIAM C. DALAND.

THE PARSONAGE, Leonardsville, N. Y., June, 1888.

# INTRODUCTION.

When he lived and reigned in Jerusalem who was "wiser than all men," then were the palmy days of God's chosen people. The kingdom, as yet undivided, enjoyed limitless peace and prosperity. Material wealth abounded as never before or since, so that the sacred historian tells us that the king made "silver and gold in Jerusalem as stones." Traders and merchant vessels brought the rarest and most costly wares from all countries. The splendor of Solomon's palace and of the temple of Jahveh is so familiar as to be proverbial. As it was a time of material grandeur, so was it also a time of literary and intellectual glory as well. Hebrew poetry had reached its golden period. The praise songs of Israel in their most perfect form were chanted by the faithful. Sage and bard wrote and sung, of earth and heaven and man, and the glory of Jahveh seemed poured forth upon His own. To the prudent son of the sweet psalmist of Israel was vouchsafed the divine gift of wisdom as never besides possessed by human soul. Wiser was he than Heman, who pierced the gloom of man's condition and saw the eternal Jahveh beneath; wiser was he than Ethan the Ezrahite, who sang of the everlasting mercies of Jahveh, and triumphed in his measure over death and Sheol. Then was accomplished the birth of Hebrew philosophy, destined to so potent an influence in the world, its germinant idea the divinely given Chokma, the beginning of which is the fear of Jahveh. To the development of this idea by the sages gathered about the king, and by those who followed after him, are we indebted for what are perhaps the most remarkable books of the Sacred Writings; namely, Job and the Song of Songs.

These books seem totally dissimilar, and yet they have much in common. They both are the product of the golden age of Hebrew literature. They both exhibit the influence of the Chokma philosophy. They both partake of a dramatic character. They are complementary the one to the other. Job depicts the experience of a man who, though in the midst of fiery trials and afflictions, has the divine gift of wisdom, the fear and perfect trust of Jahveh, which enables him to withstand them all and to come forth as the pure gold from the furnace. The Song of Songs shows us a woman who, by virtue of the same grace, is victorious over the temptations peculiar to a woman in the time of Solomon, and who remains true to her plighted troth and to her virtue, against the allurements of the most luxurious court in history.

The purpose of these books is clearly ethical, and yet their ethics, being grounded in the Chokma idea, is deeper than the ethics of nature, having its root in the "fear of Jahveh," and its consummation in the attainment of perfect character developed by the Divine Energy itself. There may have been an historical Shulamite as well as an historical Job, but both these books bear the unmistakable marks of artificiality in their external form and in their internal development. The ethical purpose of each is plainly perceived when we mark the dramatic character of the works, and when we trace the course of the argument thus presented. The details of each, both of the dramatic form and in the narratives and dialogues, show them to be works of the imagination. How much of historic fact lies beneath of course cannot be determined. It would matter not if even the basis of the narratives were fictitious; the ethical purpose would be as well subserved by an imaginary example. The dramatic character of the Song of Songs is more perfect than that of Job, though not so clearly preceptible upon the first glance, since the dialogue is continuous, and not introduced as in the book of Job by expressions indicating the person speaking. The threefold circle of speeches in Job causes its artificiality to be at once manifest, while the natural simplicity of the Song of Songs conceals its dramatic movement the more effectually. Still the fact that the most widely differing interpreters agree as to the main points of the dramatic arrangement of the poem, affords the most cogent proof that its solution is to be sought along this line. When once it is settled that the Song of Songs is a drama, and not a lyric nor a loose collection of songs, the task remaining is greatly simplified.

If it be a drama, what are the principal characters? Are there two main persons, or three? Is the poem a dialogue between Solomon and the Shulamite, with an occasional chorus, or a drama in which three principal characters figure? It would seem almost an idle question. Certainly there are two most contradictory characters to be combined into one if the whole be a dialogue between the Shulamite and one, person. A mighty king, and a humble shepherd; a rich and yet uncertain suitor, who talks of his favorite steed, his chariot, jewels, and gold, the splendor of his palace, the tower of David, shields, and weapons, and who endeavors to win affection by blandishment,—and an accepted lover, who sings of Lebanon and Amana, of ointments and spices, of springs of water, fig-trees,

and turtle-doves, of fruit, flowers, and vineyards, and
who is occupied with pastoral scenes: he who is able
to combine these exhibits far more ingenuity than is
needed to separate incongruous elements which fall
apart at the touch. Once discriminate the king in
his palace in Jerusalem from the shepherd with his
flock in the vine-clad mountain home of the Shulamite,
and the problem is solved. The changes of person,
number, and style of address reveal in most cases the
divisions of the dialogue, while the refrains, which are
so characteristic of Hebrew poetry, indicate the principal divisions of the poem.

With regard to the date and authorship of the
Song of Songs it is difficult to speak positively. The
language and style of the poem certainly point to the
age of Solomon, the golden age of Hebrew literature,
as the time when it was written. The question then
arises whether it be by Solomon, or one of the sages
of his day, or by a poet of Northern Palestine. It was
certainly written by a man used to all the scenes de-
scribed in the book, and one having an intimate ac-
quaintance with natural objects, and one familiar with
the dialect of Northern Palestine. The purpose of the
book would almost necessitate the non-Solomonic
authorship. It was assuredly written in opposition to
the profligate court of the king, though that is, of
course, not the main object of the book. It may have
been written by one of the many sages of the period.
The word "which" (*ăsher*)[1] of the title would seem to
indicate a later hand. It is in marked contrast to
the *she*[2] of the poem, and is unusual in titles, *e. g.* of
the Psalms. It was evidently added afterward by way
of statement that Solomon was the author of the book.

---

[1] אשר    [2] ש

The heroine of the drama, the Shulamite, is represented as induced to leave her vineyards and come to
the court of Solomon. He praises her beauty and by
fair words and promises endeavors to win her affection. He succeeds in gaining her attention, and
awakens in her bosom a severe struggle; but she
finally resists his advances and returns to her beloved
shepherd. It is the object of the drama to depict the
temptations peculiar to a beautiful woman brought to
the court of such a king, and to show the power of
true love to withstand them. This fidelity is genuine
virtue, and is the result of the fear of Jahveh, though
the purely dramatic character of the book hardly
permits it to declare this. Its purpose is evidently
ethical, and herein is a sufficient justification of its
place in the canon. It belongs where the other books
of the Chokma literature find a place. The treasures
of divine wisdom in the Proverbs need exemplification.
In Ecclesiastes we have the picture of a life conflict;
the deepest struggles of a noble soul are there por-
trayed, its alternations of light and darkness, hope,
belief, and skepticism made vivid and personal, but
issuing in the grand conclusion, "Fear God." In Job
we have a mighty spirit wrestling amidst darkness
and uncertainty, with that most terrible of problems,
the mysterious providence of God. With every human influence adverse, and smitten as was no man
save the Man of Sorrows, Job stands upon the firm
rock of Jahveh's integrity and proves the reality of
that wisdom which is His fear. The Song of Songs
is needed to complete the series. The most personal
of all, the most simple and natural, it has for that very
reason been misunderstood. Types, symbols, prophe-
cies, and allegories have been imagined in this book
to give it some wonderful significance, and every at-

tempt is full of inconsistencies and necessary perversions of the true meaning of the words of the poet. In this book there is as noble a soul, engaged in a struggle as momentous, with a foe as subtle and terrible as ever sacred poet has celebrated in song; and the victory is as glorious, and peradventure lies nearer the sympathy of the true human heart than that of the upright man of Uz or of Qoheleth himself. If any, however, choose to find in the Shulamite a typical reference to the Church, the Shepherd must be considered the type of Christ. Solomon would better be regarded as a type of the evil world with its allurements and snares.

The book is divided into five parts, or " acts," by the four-times recurring refrain, " I adjure you, daughters of Jerusalem," etc. Twice it is as follows:

" I adjure you, daughters of Jerusalem, by the gazelles or the hinds of the field,
That ye stir not up, nor awake love till it please."

The third time, at the end of the third act, in which is seen the climax of feeling on the part of the Shulamite, it is:

" I adjure you, daughters of Jerusalem!
Oh! that ye would find my love !
Oh! that ye would tell him that I am sick with love! "

At the close of the fourth act it is abbreviated by the omission of the words " by the gazelles or the hinds of the field." But the divisions of the poem are clearly marked by this refrain, as clearly as are the divisions in the 42d and 43d Psalms by the refrain, " Why art thou cast down," etc. When thus divided, each act is seen to have its own distinct and characteristic features. These may be indicated as follows:

Act I. ch. i. 2–ii. 7. Solomon's first attempt to

win the Shulamite from her home in Northern Palestine. Chorus of court ladies, etc.

Act II. ch. ii. 8–iii. 5. Solo of the Shulamite describing a visit of her shepherd lover. Dream of the Shulamite—she seeks her lover and finds him.

Act III. ch. iii. 6–v. 8. Second attempt of Solomon. The Shulamite has been induced to come to Jerusalem. Wedding preparations are made. Chorus of citizens of Jerusalem. Solomon's song in praise of the Shulamite. The Shulamite describes her lover as coming and courting her. Second dream of the Shulamite—she seeks her lover and fails to find him. Climax of dramatic feeling.

Act IV. ch. v. 9–viii. 4. Third attempt of Solomon. Chorus of ladies. Rustic dance. The Shulamite definitely rejects Solomon and apostrophizes her lover.

Act V. ch. viii. 5–14. Return of the Shulamite with her lover to her home. Chorus of shepherds, vinedressers, etc.

These parts, or "acts," are divided into sections, or "scenes," partly by a lesser refrain and partly by change in the action. The refrain, "my love is mine, and I am his; he feeds his flock among the lilies," occurs in different forms three times.

By exhibiting the poem in this form it is not intended to convey the impression that it was ever intended for public representation, still less that it was ever actually performed on a stage. But this form, beyond a question, best reveals the movement of the piece, and shows in a manner clearer than can be done in any other way the true significance of the book.

Some interpreters hesitate to affirm the reality of the dance in Act IV. sc. 3; but the description by the ladies certainly becomes unintelligible on any other view than that the Shulamite is there represented as actually dancing.

# PERSONS OF THE DRAMA.

THE SHULAMITE, a maiden in the vineyards of Northern Palestine.
A SHEPHERD, her lover.
SOLOMON, King in Jerusalem.
Brothers of the Shulamite, Court Ladies and Concubines of Solomon, Citizens of Jerusalem, Shepherds, Vine-dressers, etc.

---

# ARGUMENT.

The Shulamite has been induced to leave her vineyards and come to Solomon's Court. He praises her beauty and by fair words strives to win her love. He partially succeeds, but she resists his advances and goes back to her shepherd lover.

Act I. The court of King Solomon is temporarily removed to a quiet retreat in Northern Palestine. Solomon, having perceived the beauty of the Shulamite, desires to win her to be one of his wives. She is persuaded to leave her vineyards and come to the pavilion of the King. The ladies of the court, concubines of Solomon, sing in praise of the King and describe the delights of life with their royal lover, thinking thereby to influence the Shulamite to desire to join them. She, however, modestly disclaims any charms which might win the favor of Solomon, and gives expression to regret that she has left her wonted tasks to come to a place so unsuited to her. She longs to know where her lover is tending his flocks, and is smitten with the thought that to leave his companionship for the royal court is as truly desertion of her lover as it would be to have left him for one of his fellow shepherds. The ladies tell her that if she wishes her lover, she would better go back to the shepherds' tents. Solomon thereupon enters and praises her beauty. By this the Shulamite is aroused from her roving thoughts, and as a defense tells Solomon of her love for own beloved. The dialogue closes with the refrain of adjuration to the ladies not to attempt to awaken love in her unless it comes unsolicited to her bosom.

Act II.   The Shulamite then describes to the ladies a visit from her lover, dwelling upon their rural delights and the sweetness of her lover's voice as he sings to her.   Then, seeking repose, she dreams that she is taken to the city, Jerusalem, and that she goes about endeavoring to find her lover, and is successful in being reunited to him.

Act III.   The scene is now changed to Jerusalem.   Preparations have been made at the palace to receive the addition to the harem.   Marriage festivities are arranged.   The people are all out to see the pageantry.   A chorus of citizens describe Solomon's palanquin as it approaches bearing its burden of beauty.   Then in his palace Solomon once more visits the Shulamite and extols her charms in a number of wonderful similes.   The Shulamite responds no word but that she will be true to her own beloved, and avers that she would prefer her peaceful mountain home with its spice-trees to the great city with all its wealth.   Then her mind becomes excited by the peril of her situation, and her feelings rise to a climax, as she thinks of her lover coming and courting her and taking her with him.   The marriage preparations awaken this thought.   Once again she seeks repose and dreams of endeavoring to find her lover; but this time she fails, and awakens only to adjure the ladies, the only ones to whom she can appeal, to try to find her lover for her.

Act IV.   The ladies strive to soothe her by asking why she makes such an ado over her beloved; what is he more than another? The Shulamite then describes him, and becomes calmer as she proceeds.   A third time Solomon approaches her and renews his suit.   He repeats his similes and extols her above all his queens and concubines.   A scene follows in which the ladies desire to see the Shulamite execute a rustic dance for their benefit.   She accedes to their request, though modestly, and they describe her as she appears while dancing.   Solomon observes her, and enters while they are speaking, to make one more effort to persuade her; but she takes his words from his mouth and maintains the most unflinching attachment to her shepherd.   The oft repeated adjuration closes the act.

Act V.   The last act describes the return of the Shulamite to her mountain home.   A chorus of shepherds and vine-dressers welcome her.   She sings the beautiful song of love:

> " Strong as death is love ;
> Stern as Sheol is affection.
> Its flames are flames of fire,
> The flames of Jah.
> Floods cannot quench love ;
> Streams cannot sweep it away.
> If one should offer all his wealth for love,
> He would be utterly despised."

She then describes how her virtue served her to resist the blandishments of Solomon, and the drama closes with the rejoicing of the reunited lovers.

# THE SONG OF SONGS

## [WHICH IS SOLOMON'S.]

—      —

## ACT I.

SCENE. Royal Pavilion of Solomon in Northern Palestine, whither his court is moved. The Shulamite has been induced to leave her vineyards and come to the court of the king. He designs to have her among his wives.

## SCENE 1.

The Shulamite and Court Ladies, Concubines of Solomon.

*Court Lady*— Let him kiss me with his mouth's kisses,
For better are thy caresses than wine.

*Chorus of Ladies*—In fragrance thine ointments are excellent.
O ointment, " poured forth " is thy name.
Therefore do the virgins love thee.

*Court Lady*— Draw me—
*Chorus*— —after thee will we run.
*Lady*— Oh! that the king would bring me to his chambers!

*Chorus*— We will be glad; we will rejoice in thee;
We will remember thy caresses more than wine.
Rightly do they love thee.

| | |
|---|---|
| *Shulamite—* | Dark am I— |
| *Chorus—* | —but lovely— |
| *Shulamite—* | —Daughters of Jerusalem. |
| | As the tents of Kedar, |
| *Chorus—* | —as the curtains of Solomon. |

*Shulamite—*  Look not upon me, because I am dusky,
For the sun hath looked upon me.
My mother's sons were angry with me.
They made me the keeper of the vineyards,
And my vineyard, my own, I have not kept.

(*To her absent Shepherd Lover.*)

Tell me, thou whom my soul loves,
Where thou dost feed thy flocks,
Where thou dost make them rest at noon.
For why should I be as a wanderer
By the flocks of thy companions?

*Chorus—*  If thou dost not know, fairest of women,
Go forth in the foot prints of the flock,
And feed thy kids by the shepherds' tents.

## SCENE 2.

Solomon enters and praises her ; she praises her lover.

*Solomon—*  To my mare in my Pharaoh-chariot I liken thee, my dear.

Lovely are thy cheeks in rows (of
    coin), thy neck in necklaces.
Rows of gold (coin) we will make
    thee, with a pointed necklace
    of silver.

*Shulamite (aside)*—While the king was in his couch my
    nard yielded its fragrance.
*(to Solomon)* A bundle of myrrh is my love to me,
    lying between my breasts;
A cluster of henna is my love to me,
    in the vineyards of En-gedi.

*Solomon*—    Behold thou art fair, my dear,
Behold (——) thine eyes are doves.

*Shulamite*—*(to her absent lover)* Behold thou art fair, my
    love,
Yea, pleasant; our arbor is green.

*Solomon*—    The beams of our house are cedar;
Our wainscoting is of cypress.

*Shulamite*—*(to Solomon)* I am (only) the wild flower of
    Sharon,
The lily of the valleys.

*Solomon*—    As the lily among the thorns,
So is my dear among the daughters.

*Shulamite*—    As the apricot among the trees of
    the wood,
So is my love among the sons.
In his shadow I sat, delighted,
And his fruit was sweet to my taste.
Oh! that he would bring me to the
    vineyard!
His banner over me would be love.

(*to the Ladies*) Strengthen me with raisin-cakes ;
Refresh me with apricots!
For sick with love am I.

(*to Solomon*) His left hand would be under **my**
head,
And his right hand would embrace
me.

(*to the Ladies*) I adjure you, daughters of Jerusalem, by the gazelles or the
hinds of the field,
That ye stir not up, nor awake love
till it please.

## ACT II.

SCENE. The same as in Act I.

### SCENE 1.—(Ideal.)

Solo of the Shulamite describing a visit of her lover.

*Shulamite—* Hark! my love! see there! he comes!
Leaping over the mountains, bound-
ing over the hills.
My love is like a gazelle or a fawn.
See there! he is standing behind our
walls,
Looking in from the windows, gleam-
ing through the lattice.'
My love doth sing forth, he says to
me:—
" Rise up, my dear, my fair one, and
come away.
For see, the winter is past ;
The rain has glided away—has gone

The blossoms appear in the earth;
The time of song has approached,
And the voice of the turtle-dove is
    heard in our land.
The fig tree is spicy with its figs,
And the vines in blossom yield fra-
    grance.
Rise up, my dear, my fair one, and
    come away."
My dove is in the clefts of the rock,
    . in the recesses of the cliffs.
Let me see thy countenance; let me
    hear thy voice.
For thy voice is sweet, and thy coun-
    tenance is lovely.
" Take us the jackals, the little jack-
    als,
The spoilers of our vineyards, for
    our vineyards are in blossom."
My love is mine, and I am his; he
    feeds his flock among the lilies.
Until the day breathes, and the shad-
    ows flee, go about;
Be, O my love, like a gazelle (———)
    on the mountains of Bether.

### SCENE 2.--(Ideal.)

**Dream of the Shulamite.   She seeks her lover and finds him.**

*Shulamite—*    Upon my bed in the dark night I
    sought (him)—
Him whom my soul loves.
I sought him, but found him not.
(I said) " I will arise and go about
    in the city.

In the streets and the broad ways I
    will seek (him)—
Him whom my soul loves."
I sought him, but found him not.
The watchmen who go about the city
    found me.
(I said) " Him whom my soul loves
    have you seen?"
Scarcely had I passed on from them
When I found him whom my soul
    loves.
I seized him and would not release
    him,
Until I had brought him unto the
    house of my mother,
And to the chamber of her that con-
    ceived me.

*(to the Ladies)* I adjure you, daughters of Jerusa-
    lem, by the gazelles or the
    hinds of the field,
That ye stir not up, nor awake love
    till it please.

---

## ACT III.

SCENE. Jerusalem. A street and palace of Solomon. The Shulamite
has been induced to come thither. Wedding preparations are made.

## SCENE 1.

Bridal procession in the street. Chorus of citizens.

*Chorus—*        Who there, is coming up from the
    wilderness,
Like pillars of smoke — incense,
    myrrh, and frankincense—

Out of all the aromatics of the merchant?

*1st Citizen* (*solo*)— See there! his palanquin, Solomon's
Sixty mighty men around it, of the heroes of Israel.
They all lay hold of swords, trained in battle,
Each one with his sword at his side for fear in the night.

*2d Citizen* (*solo*)— A palanquin King Solomon made him of the wood of Lebanon.
Its pillars he made of silver,
Its railings of gold, its cushion of purple,
Its interior adorned with the one beloved above the daughters of Jerusalem.

*Chorus*— Go forth and look, O daughters of Zion,
At King Solomon with the crown wherewith his mother crowned him,
In the day of his nuptials, the day his heart is glad.

## SCENE 2.

Solomon visits the Shulamite in his palace and praises her beauty.

*Solomon*— Behold thou art fair, my dear, behold thou art fair.
Thine eyes are doves from between thy locks.
Thy hair is like a flock of she-goats that glisten from Mount Gilead.

Thy teeth are like a flock of shorn
sheep which come up from
washing,

Of which all bear twins; and not one
among them is sterile.

Like a crimson thread are thy lips,
and thy mouth is lovely.

Like a slice of pomegranate are thy
temples between thy locks.

Like the tower of David is thy neck,
built for an armory;

A thousand shields hang upon it, all
shields of heroes.

Thy two breasts are like two fawns,
twins of the gazelle.

Thou art all fair, my dear, in thee is
no blemish.

*Shulamite—*

(My love is mine, and I am his); he
feeds his flock among the
lilies.

Until the day breathes, and the
shadows flee,

I will go to the mountain of myrrh
and the hill of frankincense.

### SCENE 3.—(Probably Ideal.)

The Shulamite, excited, thinks of her lover as coming and courting her
and defying Solomon.   Marriage preparations suggest her thought.

*Shepherd—*

" With me from Lebanon, my bride,
with me from Lebanon do
thou come.

Do thou look from the top of Amana,
from the top of Shenir and
Hermon,

From the dens of lions, from the
mountains of leopards.
Thou hast taken away my heart, my
sister, my bride, thou hast
taken away my heart,
With one of thine eyes, with one
chain of thy neck.
How lovely are thy caresses, my
sister, my bride ;
How much better are thy caresses
than wine,
And the fragrance of thine ointments than all spices!
Thy lips, my bride, drip with honey;
Honey and milk are under thy
tongue,
And the fragrance of thy garments
is like the fragrance of Lebanon.
A garden barred is my sister, my
bride,
A spring shut up, a fountain sealed.
Thy plants are a park of pomegranates with most precious fruit,
Henna with spices, nard and saffron,
Sweet reed and cinnamon with all
frankincense trees,
Myrrh and aloes with all the chief
spices.
A garden spring (art thou), a well
of living water, and streams
of Lebanon."

*Shulamite—*

Awake thou north wind, and come
thou south wind.

Blow upon my garden that its spices
    may flow.
Let my love come into his garden,
    and eat his precious fruit.

*Shepherd—*

" I am come to my garden, my sister,
    my bride;
I have gathered my myrrh with my
    spice;
I have eaten my honey-drippings
    with my honey;
I have drunk my wine with my
    milk——
*(Aside)* Eat, O friends, drink and be drunk-
    en."

## SCENE 4.—(Ideal.)

Second dream of the Shulamite.  She fails to find her lover.

*Shulamite—*

I sleep, but my heart is awake.
Hark! my love! knocking (and say-
    ing)
" Open to me, my sister, my dear, my
    dove, my perfect one.
For my head is filled with dew, and
    my locks with the drops of the
    night."
" I have put off my garment; how
    shall I put it on?
I have washed my feet; how shall I
    defile them?"
My love put in his hand at the door-
    hole,
And I was inwardly moved for him.
I rose to open to my love and my
    hands dropped myrrh,

And my fingers with flowing myrrh
    upon the handles of the lock.
I opened to my love,
But my love had withdrawn—he
    was gone.
My soul went forth when he spoke;
I sought him, but found him not.
I called to him, but he did not an-
    swer me.
The watchmen, going about the city,
    found me.
They smote me; they wounded me.
The keepers of the walls took away
    my mantle.
(*to the Ladies*) I adjure you, daughters of Jerusa-
    lem!
Oh! that ye would find my love!
Oh! that ye would tell him that I am
    sick with love!

## ACT IV.

SCENE. The same as in Act III. Palace of Solomon.

### SCENE 1.

Dialogue between the Court Ladies and the Shulamite regarding her beloved.

*Chorus of Ladies*—What is thy love more than (any)
    love, fairest of women?
    What is thy love more than (any)
    love, that thou shouldest so
    adjure us?

*Shulamite*—My love is sunny and ruddy, banner
    bearer among myriads.

His head is fine gold;
His locks are bushy, black as a ra-
ven.
His eyes are as doves by the water
brooks,
Bathing in milk, dwelling by full
fountains.
His cheeks are as a bed of spices pro-
ducing aromatic plants.
His lips are lilies, dripping with
flowing myrrh.
His hands are rods of gold filled
with jewels.
His body is ivory work covered over
with sapphires.
His legs are pillars of marble set on
bases of gold.
His face is like Lebanon, choice as
the cedars.
His mouth is most sweet; he is alto-
gether precious.
This is my love, and this my dear
one, O daughters of Jerusalem.

*Chorus of Ladies*—Whither has thy love gone, fairest
of women?
Whither has thy love gone, that we
may seek him with thee?

*Shulamite*— My love has gone down to his garden,
to the beds of spices,
To feed his flocks in the gardens,
and to gather lilies.
I am my love's and my love is mine;
he feeds his flock among the
lilies.

## SCENE 2.

Solomon enters and praises her beauty.

*Solomon*—
Fair art thou, my dear, as Tirzah,
Lovely as Jerusalem, awe-inspiring
    as a bannered host.
Turn away thine eyes from me, for
    they have conquered me.
Thy hair is like a flock of she-goats
    that glisten from Mount Gil-
    ead.
Thy teeth are like a flock of shorn
    sheep which come up from
    washing.
Of which all bear twins; and not one
    among them is sterile.
Like a slice of pomegranate are thy
    temples between thy locks.
Threescore are the queens, and four-
    score the concubines,
And virgins without number.
One is my dove, my perfect one;
She is the only one of her mother,
The choice one of her who bare her.
The daughters saw her and blessed
    her;
The queens and the concubines, and
    they praised her.

## SCENE 3.

Chorus of Ladies admiring the Shulamite and urging her to dance. She does so, and they describe her movements and her person as disclosed in the dance.

*Chorus of Ladies*—Who is this that looketh forth as the
    dawn,

Fair as the moon, clear as the sun,
Awe-inspiring as a bannered host?

Shulamite— Unto the nut garden I went down to
see the fruit of the valley,
To see if the vine budded and the
pomegranate blossomed.
Before I knew it my soul made me
chariots of Ammi-Nadib.

Chorus— Turn! turn! O Shulamite!
Turn! turn! that we may look upon
thee.
Shulamite— What would ye see in the Shulamite?
Chorus— The dance of Mahanaim.
Chorus— How beautiful are thy steppings in
shoes, O noble one!
Thy rounded thighs are like jewels,
the work of an artist's hands.
Thy turnings are circular movements; let them not lack variation.
Thy body is a sheaf of wheat, set
about with lilies.
Thy two breasts are like two fawns,
twins of the gazelle.
Thy neck is like a tower of ivory.
Thine eyes are the pools in Heshbon,
by the gate of Bath-Rabbim.
Thy nose is like the tower of Lebanon, looking forth toward Da-
mascus.
Thy head upon thee is like Carmel,
and the locks of thy head like
purple (black).

A king is taken in thy tresses————

*Enter Solomon.*

## SCENE 4.

Solomon again approaches her; but she discloses an unflinching attachment to her beloved Shepherd.

*Solomon—*  How fair art thou, and how pleasant, O love, in delights!

This thy stature is like to a palmtree and thy breasts to clusters.

I said: " I will climb the palm, I will take hold of its branches.

And thy breasts shall be as clusters of the vine,

And the fragrance of thy nose like apricots,

And thy mouth like the best wine ————"

*Shulamite (interrupting)* Flowing sweetly for my love, flowing gently (down) the lips of sleepers.

I am my love's and for me is his desire.

*(to her absent Lover)* Come, my love, let us go forth to the field, let us lodge in the villages.

Let us arise early to the vineyard; let us see whether the vine sprouts,

(Whether) its blossom opens, (whether) the pomegranates bloom.

There will I give thee my caresses.

The mandrakes yield their scent;
And at our gates are all precious
    fruits new and old,
(Which), my love, I have laid up for
    thee.
Oh! that thou wert as my brother,
    who sucked the breasts of my
    mother!
(When) I found thee without I would
    kiss thee,
And they would surely not despise
    me.
I would lead thee, I would bring thee
    to my mother's house; she
    would teach me;
I would give thee drink of the spiced
    wine of my pomegranate juice.
*(to the Ladies)* His left hand would be under my
    head, and his right hand would
    embrace me.
I adjure you, daughters of Jerusa-
    lem—
That ye stir not up nor awake love
    till it please.

## ACT V.

SCENE. Mountain home of the Shulamite in Northern Palestine.

### SCENE 1.

Shulamite on the arm of her lover. Chorus of Shepherds, Vine-dressers, etc.

*Chorus—* Who is this coming up from the wil-
    derness,

Leaning upon her love?

*Shulamite—* Under the apricot tree I awakened
    thy love.
There thy mother brought thee
    forth;
There she that brought thee forth
    bare thee.
Place me as a seal upon thy heart,
As a seal upon thy hand.
For strong as death is love;
Stern as Sheol is affection.
Its flames are flames of fire,
The flames of Jah.
Floods cannot quench love;
Streams cannot sweep it away.
If one should offer all his wealth for
    love,
He would be utterly despised.

## SCENE 2.

Shulamite and her Brothers, etc.

*Brothers—* We have a little sister and she is not
    matured.
What shall we do for our sister when
    she is asked in marriage?
If she were a wall, we would build
    upon her a silver castle;
If she were a door, we would carve
    upon her a cedar tablet.

*Shulamite—* I am a wall, and my breasts like tow-
    ers.
Then was I in his eyes as one that
    found peace.

Solomon had a vineyard in Baal
    Hamon.
He gave the vineyard to keepers;
Each for its fruit used to bring a
    thousand of silver.
My vineyard, my own, is before me.
Thou, O Solomon, hast a thousand,
    and two hundred fruit-keep-
    ers.

*Shepherd Lover—* Thou that dwellest in the gardens,
The companions listen to thy voice;
Let me hear it.

*Shulamite—* Break away, my love, and be like a
    gazelle,
Or a fawn on the mountains of spices.

[THE END.]

# TABLE OF DIVISIONS

*Note.* These divisions are according to the numbering of the Hebrew Bible. Following the English Bible, read:

# NOTES.

*TITLE.* **The Song of Songs, which is Solomon's**. The word *'asher* (which) indicates a later hand. The proper title of the poem is the Song of Songs, *i. e.*, the most beautiful, or excellent, of songs.

## ACT I.

*SCENE* 1. **Let him kiss me,** etc. One of the ladies (solo) speaks of her desire for the king's caresses.

**In fragrance,** etc. The chorus of ladies continue in praise of Solomon.

**O ointment,** evidently a term of endearment. Compare " my nard," Sc. 2, *Shulamite (aside)*. Also compare Job xlii. 14, *Qeren Chappûkh*, paint horn, *i. e.*, cosmetic box.

**Draw me—after thee will we run.** The change to number here shows that the chorus interrupt.

**Dark am I—but lovely**—etc. A striking and beautiful passage in which there is clearly a similar interruption by the chorus. The court ladies have engaged in converse about the joys they have had with Solomon, in order to move the Shulamite to yield to him. She then speaks of her sun-burned hue as unworthy of their attention. " Dark am I," she says, " as the tents of Kedar; " " but lovely," say the ladies, " as the curtains of Solomon." The Shulamite then proceeds to lament her neglect in leaving her tasks and coming with the ladies to Solomon's pavilion.

**Tell me. thou whom my soul loves.** Here the Shulamite apostrophizes her absent lover, and signifies her sorrow at having wandered away. She remembers that she would never have left her lover for another of his own station, and her conduct now appears to her mind in its true light.

**If thou dost not know.** The ladies are irritated to think that no greater impression has been made upon the Shulamite, and they impatiently tell her to go out and follow the tracks of the flocks, if she prefers such a life to the luxurious one to which they would lead her.

*SCENE* 2. **To my mare**. Solomon now begins a characteristic dialogue by comparing the beautiful maiden to his favorite steed.

**In my Pharaoh-chariot.** Literally "In my chariot of Pharaoh," or possibly "in Pharaoh's chariots," though the latter would not be so intelligible. The Hebrew expression here[1] may be pointed so as to read *Berikhbî Phar 'ôh* just as readily as *Berikhebhê Phar 'ôh*. It requires a change of but two vowel points. That a closeness of relation, like the above, may exist between words even when the first has the pronominal suffix is seen from passages like Ezek. xvi. 27, Psa. lxxi. 7, etc. The chariot may have been one from Egypt so called (see 2 Chron. i. 16, 17), or perhaps it may have been a gift from the Pharaoh with whom Solomon had made an alliance. 1 Kings iii. 1.

**Lovely are thy cheeks**, etc. The Eastern women adorn themselves with bronze coins and necklaces. Solomon promises the Shulamite ornaments of gold and silver instead.

**While the king was in his couch**. The coming of the king from his place of retirement disturbed the Shulamite in her thoughts of her lover. Until the appearance of Solomon those thoughts had been to her as agreeable as the fragrance of nard, which epithet she applies to her lover. Compare "O ointment," Sc. 1, *Chorus of ladies*.

**A bundle of myrrh**, etc. A careful rendering of this passage relieves it of any impropriety. The Shulamite simply compares her lover to a packet of aromatics which she wore upon her person as a perfume, a not uncommon practice among ladies of the East. (See Isa. iii. 20, *bottê hannephesh, i. e.,* scent boxes.) The parallel comparison of her lover to a cluster of henna in the vineyards of En-gedi, shows that the verb refers to the situation of the packet of myrrh and not to that of the lover.

**My love**. This word, *dôdh*, is the one continually recurring throughout the poem, employed by the Shulamite as the special

designation of her beloved. It is used of one beloved, also for a
friend, or relation (uncle), Isa. v. 1, Lev. x. 4. 1 Sam. x. 14, Esth. ii.
15, etc. In the plural (*dôdhîm*) it signifies caresses, tokens of love,
as in Act I. Sc. 1 (ch. i. 2 and 4) and Act III. Sc. 3 (ch. iv. 10).
But in Act III. Sc. 3 (ch. v. 1) it also signifies *friends*.

**Behold thou art fair, my dear,**

**Behold (——) thine eyes are doves.**

The rhythm in Hebrew is made much more in accord with the general metrical arrangement if the word *japhah* be omitted the second
time. It may have come in here accidentally on account of the similarity to Act III. Sc. 2.

Note that the words of Solomon here and throughout the poem
are in marked contrast with those of the Shulamite. Compare
their words when she speaks of her lover to offset Solomon's language, *e. g.*, " mare," " chariot," " necklaces," " beams," " wainscoting," etc., with " myrrh," " henna," and " green " boughs.

**I am (only) the wild flower of Sharon,** said modestly and without reference to beauty or grace. The flower, *chă-
bhatstseleth*, is a simple autumnal flower, growing in meadows,
resembling a crocus. Sharon is either a plain *(sharôn)* in general,
or the particular strip of plain country near the Mediterranean so
called. It is either " the wild flower of the plain," or " the wild flower of Sharon."

**Oh! that he would bring me to the vineyard!**
Vineyard (*bêth hajjajin*), *i. e.*, the *place whence wine comes*, is better than " banqueting house." The Hebrew word *bêth*, a noun of
relation, does not always mean house; in fact it oftener has the
meaning of place in a general sense. See compounds, Josh. x. 11,
2 Sam. x. 6, etc. Thus the language of the Shulamite becomes
more natural and in accord with her thought.

**Strengthen me with raisin-cakes,** *i. e.*, pressed grapes
(*'ăshîshôth*); compare Hos. iii. 1.

**I adjure you, daughters of Jerusalem**, etc. The
thought of this refrain is that the ladies are not to attempt to arouse
in the heart of the Shulamite any feeling in response to that of Solomon. Love, if it come to her bosom at all, must come unsolicited.

## ACT II.

*SCENE* 1.—(*Ideal.*) The scenes marked *Ideal* are either entirely ideal, merely showing what passes in the mind of the Shulamite, or ideal in so far as the lover is concerned, and the Shulamite simply relates her dreams, etc., to the ladies. From the way in which Act IV. opens. it would seem that Act III. Sc. 4, was certainly related by the Shulamite to her auditors, the ladies. These deal scenes could not well be represented upon a stage. It may be best to regard them all as narrated by the Shulamite to the ladies.

**Hark! my love! see there! he comes!** The Shulamite vividly describes a visit of her lover. Note the simplicity and beauty of the references to objects of nature. She represents her lover as singing to her.

**Take us the jackals, the little jackals.** This is probably a snatch of a familiar song her lover used to sing, and which she imagines him singing. The line before speaks of his voice as sweet, and naturally leads to the quotation.

**Be, O my love, like a gazelle (———) on the mountains of Bether.** The words omitted here probably crept in on account of the similarity of this passage with the distich at the close of Act V. Sc. 2. The line here is too long in the Hebrew to accord with the general metrical arrangement. The omission of these words restores what was probably the original line.

*SCENE* 2.—(*Ideal.*) **Upon my bed in the dark night,** etc. This scene describes a dream of the Shulamite, which she relates to the ladies. In her dream she imagines that having been taken to the city, she wanders about there in search of her lover. In her vision she finds him, and they are reunited in her own home. The peaceful conclusion of the dream gives her strength, and she adjures the ladies as at the close of Act I. The word night (*lêlôth*) in the first line is in the plural. indicating an intensification of the idea of the word, hence *dark* night.

## ACT III.

*SCENE* 1. **Who there, is coming up from the wilderness,** etc. Notice the boldness of this piece, and its vigorous style, also the symmetry of its structure.

**See there! his palanquin, Solomon's.** The word here is not the same as the one similarly translated in the solo of the second citizen, but they are the same in effect. The word here (*mittah*) means *that upon which one may recline, i. e.*, a bed; but it is used of a bier in 2 Sam. iii. 31, where it is clear that it was a litter to be carried from place to place. The word below (*'appir-iôn*) means *that which may be borne* from place to place, hence a litter. The word palanquin expresses, therefore, the idea of both words, and it will be seen from the context that they both refer to the same object.

**Its interior adorned with the one beloved,** etc. *Adorned*—literally, paved, tesselated; but of course for the sake of beauty. *The one beloved*, a concrete use of the word love (*'ahâbhâh*) with which compare the same word in Act IV. Sc. 4 (ch. vii. 7— English Bible 6). The finishing touch to the palanquin is given by the beauty of its occupant.

*SCENE 2.* **Behold thou art fair, my dear.** etc. Notice the similes in this piece. The king gives free rein to his imagination, and fairly revels in imagery. He begins with figures which the Shulamite can appreciate, and advances to the "tower of David" with its "thousand shields." This song is a beautiful poem by itself, beginning and ending with almost the same words, a not uncommon form in Hebrew poetry Compare Psa. viii. 2 and 10— English Bible 1 and 9.

**(My love is mine and I am his,)** etc. If we compare the refrain at the close of this scene with the conclusion of Act II. Sc. 1, it will appear that in chapter iv. verse 7 and the last part of verse 5 must be transposed. If then we supply the missing words, "My love is mine and I am his," we shall have a refrain quite similar to that in chapter ii. verses 16 and 17. Furthermore this transposition causes Solomon's piece here to begin and end with the same expression. All these changes cause the lines of poetry to become equalized and more metrical in the Hebrew. Apparently the poem has here suffered a little from the ravages of time.

*SCENE 3.—(Probably Ideal.)* **With me from Lebanon, my bride,** etc. The preparations for the marriage cause the Shulamite in her excited state to think of her lover as coming and courting her. It is a matter of dispute whether this scene be real or ideal. It is, however, probably ideal, and is intended to represent merely what passes in the mind of the Shulamite. Compare this with the description of the visit in Act II. Sc. 1, and notice that a dream follows in Sc. 2, just as here in Act III. Sc. 4. It is better, therefore, to regard this as the product of the vivid imagination of the Shulamite wrought upon by the circumstances of her condition.

Observe the difference between this piece and Solomon's song in Sc. 2. Notice the free and natural use of imagery here. Solomon's piece is a finely polished and exquisitely finished description, every simile studied with care. This one is infinitely less artificial, and more in keeping with the character of the Shepherd. There is a great difference also in the matter itself. The King views nature in her artificial aspect under the influence of civilization; the Shepherd sees nature in her primitive wildness. The king speaks of a "crimson thread," a "*slice* of pomegranate," a "tower," with "shields," etc.; the Shepherd talks of "honey and milk," "pomegranates," *au naturel*, "dens of lions," "mountains of leopards," etc. The references of the Shepherd and the Shulamite are to their own customary mode of life in its rural simplicity; Solomon's reference is to nature under the view of the art critic.

(*Aside*) **Eat, O friends, drink and be drunken.** The imagination of the Shulamite is carried forward to her own marriage with her lover. These words are an exhortation on the part of the Shepherd to the guests. This renders it certain that this scene is ideal and not real. The thought is of what the Shepherd *would have said*, if it were his wedding, and not that he did really come to Jerusalem and say and do as here is indicated. The strong language, "drink and be drunken," may be referred to the excitement of the occasion,

*SCENE* 4.—(*Ideal.*) **I sleep, but my heart is awake**, *i. e.*, I dream. Compare this dream with the one in Act II. Sc. 2. The difference between the peaceful conclusion of the first dream and the tumultuous close of this one is to be referred to the excitement of the Shulamite in view of the peril of her condition. Observe the unfortunate details in this dream.

**My love put in his hand at the door-hole,** *i. e.,* the aperture in the door of Eastern houses through which a person from without may put his hand to unfasten the bar or pin which secures the door.

**I rose to open to my love, and my hands dropped myrrh.** This passage illustrates the use of ointments by Eastern women.

**My soul went forth,** *i. e.,* I went forth. The word soul (*nephesh*) with the pronominal suffixes (*naphshî,* etc.,) is used continually in Hebrew in the sense of *self;* compare " him whom my soul loves," (*i. e.,* whom *I* love) in Act II. Sc. 2, Compare also Psa. xvi. 10.

**I adjure you, daughters of Jerusalem!** Here we have a variation in the refrain caused by the climax of dramatic feeling. The Shulamite knows not whither to look for help, but to her lover. She is about to be driven into yielding to Solomon's entreaties, and in her helplessness she appeals to the ladies to find her lover, that he may come and rescue her.

### ACT IV.

*SCENE* 1. **What is thy love more than (any) love, fairest of women?** The ladies become weary of her adjurations and desire to know what there is in her beloved Shepherd that makes him so desirable.

**My love is sunny and ruddy,** etc. Here we have a beautiful description of the Shepherd The Shulamite now derives her imagery from the treasures she has seen. She seizes upon figures drawn from the costly and rare jewels and the magnificent carved work she has observed in Solomon's palace. Contrast this with her words in Act I., before she was brought to Jerusalem, and observe how her changed situation finds its reflection in her language.

*SCENE* 2. **Fair art thou, my dear, as Tirzah,** etc. Solomon enters and renews his suit. He compares the Shulamite to Tirzah and Jerusalem, the former a beautiful town in Northern Palestine, and the latter his capital and royal residence. But he also finds her somewhat inaccessible, " awe-inspiring as a bannered host." He then returns to his former similes, and, having exhausted his images, is driven to compare her with his queens and concubines to their disadvantage.

*SCENE* 3. **Who is this that looketh forth as the dawn,** etc. By this time the ladies are naturally enough thoroughly weary of the affair; still they continue to praise the Shulamite, and employ Solomon's comparison with possibly a little concealed sarcasm.

**Before I knew it my soul made me chariots of Ammi-Nadib.** In her thoughts the maiden is borne away to the scene of her home with its tasks. Her mind has swiftly conveyed her as a chariot would have done. The word Ammi-Nadib is somewhat obscure. Literally it would seem to mean, "my people, the noble." It may mean "the people of the prince." The expression then would be "the chariots of the people of the prince." Still Ammi-Nadib may be a proper name. Compare Amminadab. Ex. vi. 23. However, the idea conveyed by the whole sentence is clear enough, no matter what be the significance of this expression. Swift thought served to transport the Shulamite to her home, just as the royal chariots would have done.

**Turn! turn! O Shulamite!**

**Turn! turn! that we may look upon thee.**

Here we have the ladies urging the Shulamite to dance for their entertainment. The description which follows clearly indicates this. The word Shulamite (*Shûlammîth*) is a proper name from Shunem, or Shulem. The word is probably a dialectic variation of Shunammite (*Shûnammîth*, 1 Kings i. 3, 2 Kings iv. 12 and 25.) The article in the Hebrew shows that this is not the proper name of the maiden herself. Some have so taken it, deriving the word as the feminine form of Solomon, but the article would hardly thus be used with the name of the maiden. The town mentioned above (*Shûnêm*, or *Sûlêm*) is evidently indicated as the place to which her abode is to be referred. It is called Σουλήμ by Eusebius, and the modern *Sôlam* is probably its equivalent.

**The dance of Mahanaim.** Exactly what this means is not clear. Some interpreters connect these words with the previous question. So the Revisers render: "Why will ye look upon the Shulamite as upon the dance of Mahanaim?" But it is better to regard these words as the natural answer to the question. Whether there is here a reference to Gen. xxxii. 1–3, perhaps may not reasonably be doubted; but, whatever be the meaning intended by Mahanaim, it is certain that the ladies desired to see the Shulamite dance some sort of a dance for their benefit. That she is actually represented as dancing is clearly indicated by the first line of the succeeding description. Only prejudice can account for any other view.

**How beautiful are thy steppings in shoes, O noble one!** Steps or steppings (*pe'âmajikh*), not "feet" as in the A. V. "Noble one," better expresses the thought of the Hebrew use of *bath*, a noun of relation. The poem does not represent the Shulamite as the daughter of a prince. The words son and daughter are constantly used in Hebrew to designate persons possessing characteristics indicated by the word in connection with which they are used. " Daughter of Belial " (*bath belijja'al*), 1 Sam. i. 16, means "daughter of wickedness," *i. e.*, a "wicked woman." " Son of uprightness" (*ben chajil*), 1 Kings i. 52, is properly translated a "worthy man." So here, "daughter of a noble " means a "noble woman."

**Thy turnings are circular movements; let them not lack variation** Here is a reference to the turning of the Shulamite in the dance. The word translated in the A. V. "navel" (*shorer*) is a participial form of a verb (*shârar*) meaning, to turn, to twist, to twine, *to go in a circle*. This form is only used here and elsewhere when the navel is mentioned (Prov. iii. 8, Job xl. 16, and Ezek. xvi. 4) different forms, derived from the same root, are used. Here the form is that of the active participle, and would signify a turning, a revolving, or a going in a circle, rather than a thing twisted. Furthermore this accords better with the idea of the dance, and is more in keeping with the whole description. The word translated in the A. V. "goblet" (*'aggân*) is ~~probably~~ a trough for washing, hence a laver, or any bowl or vessel. It is derived from a root (*'âghan*) signifying *to tread with the feet*, hence to wash clothes (by treading or stamping), whence the significance of laver for the noun. Now, if we here return to the original idea of the root, we shall get a meaning more suited to this description. Instead of "a round goblet" (A. V.) we have "a circular treading of the feet," beyond question a reference to the dance. To compare the navel to a round goblet, or even a round washing-trough (*sic!*) is hardly a fit reference. It is wanting in sense, as well as in modesty and beauty. But the reference to the circular treading of the Shulamite in the dance is natural, and fully in harmony with the other parts of the description: To apply the term navel to the part of the Shulamite's person *around the navel*, as is done by most interpreters, even (and especially) if clothed and adorned with a jeweled girdle, is to employ a synechdoche which is unnatural and forced. The word translated in the A. V. " liquor" (*mezegh*) means *mixture*, hence "mixed wine," if in a goblet. But in view of the previous reference it would more naturally signify variations or alterations in the dance. The ladies desire her to continue the dance and to introduce into her movements as much "mixture" or variety as possible. The verbal expression, '*al-jech-sar*, is the regular Hebrew use in prohibitions or deprecations, " let not." The Revisers render:

> " Thy navel is like a round goblet
> Wherein no mingled wine is wanting."

The second line should certainly be:

> " In it let no mingled wine be wanting."

But in accord with the general spirit of the piece it is better to render the whole consistently, thus: "Thy turnings are circular movements; let them not lack variation." This rendering is pleasing and natural, and in every way more satisfactory.

**Thine eyes are the pools in Heshbon, by the gate of Bath-Rabbim.** Heshbon, modern *Hesbân*, near which are remains of masonry belonging to at least one such pool, was the city of the Kings of Moab (Deut. ii. 24–37, Num. xxi. 25–35). The pools mentioned must have been near the gate of that city, which is designated as *Bath-Rabbim*, literally " daughter of multitudes," *i. e.*, a populous city; or perhaps *Bath-Rabbim* is a designation of a particular gate, the gate where markets and tribunals (hence *multitudes*) were held. " Daughter " is a term often applied to cities— Isa. i. 8, x. 32, Ps. cxxxvii. 8, Zech. ii. 11—English Bible ii. 7.

**A king is taken in thy tresses**—The word here used (*r^ehâtîm*) means ringlets or curls, so called from their *flowing*. The root (*râhat*) means to run or flow, as water. An interruption is here made by Solomon, who enters and observes the Shulamite. Hence the ladies refer to him as charmed by her beauty. The last line is broken and unfinished, thus showing the interruption.

*SCENE* 4. **How fair art thou, and how pleasant, O love, in delights!** Thus Solomon begins his address. The word here translated " love " (*'ahâbhâh*) is the ordinary word used in this poem for love, *e. g.*, ch. ii. 4, ch. viii. 6, 7. It is the word

— 49 —

used in the refrain which closes each act, ch. ii. 7, ch. iii. 5, ch. v. 8, and ch. viii. 4. Here (ch. vii. 7—English Bible 6,) and in Act III. Sc. 1 (ch. iii. 10) it is used in a concrete sense of "one beloved." This is not the continually recurring word employed by the Shulamite to designate her beloved.

**Flowing sweetly for my love, Flowing gently (down) the lips of sleepers.** The Shulamite here interrupts Solomon, and gives him to understand that the charms he praises are for her lover only.

## ACT V.

*SCENE* 1. **Who is this?** etc. Compare the chorus of citizens in Act III. Sc. 1.

**Under the apricot tree,** etc. The lovers are now reunited in their old home where they both were born and reared. The victory of true love over all the allurements of the great city and the royal court is now strikingly related,

**For strong as death is love;**
**Stern as Sheol is affection.**

This is a beautiful song of love. Love is represented as firm as death and as relentless as Sheol, the abode of the dead. Its flames are divine flames which naught can quench. All the wealth that the great king could offer were despised by the true heart of one who possessed this treasure, a pure and loyal affection.

*SCENE* 2. **We have a little sister,** etc. The Shulamite's brothers are speaking of her as young and tender, needing their protection. They know not how to defend her. Were she a wall or a door, the mode of procedure would be clear; but as she is only a maiden they cannot tell what course to pursue. This is to introduce the declaration which follows. They do not know what the power of love and the influence of trial have been in developing the character of their little vineyard-keeper.

**I am a wall,** etc. Her virtue has proven to her a power of defence in a time of the severest ordeal. After speaking of this, the Shulamite contrasts Solomon's great vineyard near Baal-Hamon (perhaps a town in Samaria, *Βελαμών*, Judith viii. 3), its many fruit keepers and rich vintage, with her own humble dwelling; and the suggestion is of Solomon's wealth and his harem, in contrast to her obscure but faithful Shepherd.

**Thou that dwellest in the gardens,** etc. Here is given a tender complaint of the lover that the Shulamite is giving too much attention to her friends and kindred, her companions. He wants her to himself.

**Break away my love and be like a gazelle.** This refrain, sung by the Shulamite, closes the poem, which ends in the joy of a triumphant victory over the insidious foe who would have destroyed the purity and peace of two loyal and loving hearts.

AMERICAN SABBATH TRACT SOCIETY  STEAM PRINT, ALFRED CENTRE, N. Y.